This book belongs to ...

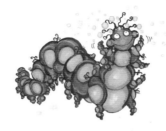

For my daughter, Linette, who discovered the beetle in our bathroom

And for all her friends at Little Ridge School, St Leonards on Sea

B. M.

For Jacob

S. H.

Beetle
in the
Bathroom

PUFFIN BOOKS

Published by the Penguin Group
Penguin Books Ltd, 80 Strand, London WC2R 0RL, England
Penguin Putnam Inc., 375 Hudson Street, New York, New York 10014, USA
Penguin Books Australia Ltd, 250 Camberwell Road, Camberwell, Victoria 3124, Australia
Penguin Books Canada Ltd, 10 Alcorn Avenue, Toronto, Ontario, Canada M4V 3B2
Penguin Books India (P) Ltd, 11 Community Centre, Panchsheel Park, New Delhi – 110 017, India
Penguin Books (NZ) Ltd, Cnr Rosedale and Airborne Roads, Albany, Auckland, New Zealand
Penguin Books (South Africa) (Pty) Ltd, 24 Sturdee Avenue, Rosebank 2196, South Africa

Penguin Books Ltd, Registered Offices: 80 Strand, London WC2R 0RL

www.penguin.com

First published 2001
9 10

Text copyright © Brian Moses, 2001
Illustrations copyright © Sonia Holleyman, 2001
All rights reserved

The moral right of the author and illustrator has been asserted

Manufactured in China

British Library Cataloguing in Publication Data
A CIP catalogue record for this book is available from the British Library

ISBN-13: 978-0-14056-704-5
ISBN-10: 0-14056-704-6

Beetle in the Bathroom

Brian Moses and Sonia Holleyman

PUFFIN BOOKS

When I peeped around

the bathroom door

I couldn't believe the
things I saw ...

A caterpillar was
washing his hair

with my shampoo –

I don't think that's fair.

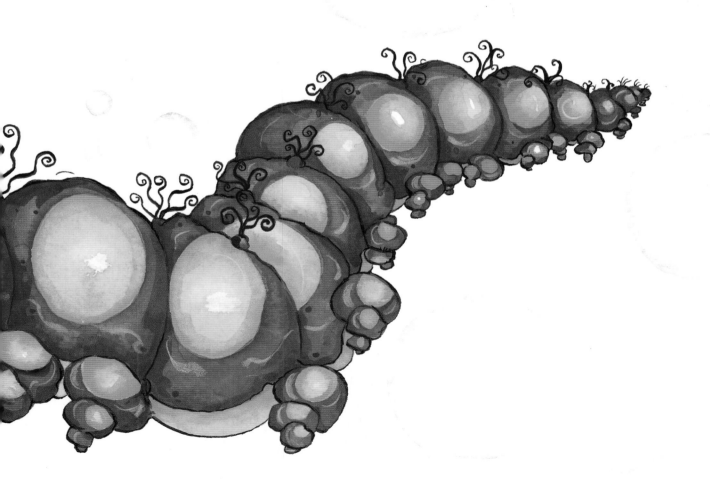

A woodlouse saw me
and started to wave.

A ladybird was skiing

a zigzag path

down the smooth and

slippery sides of our bath.

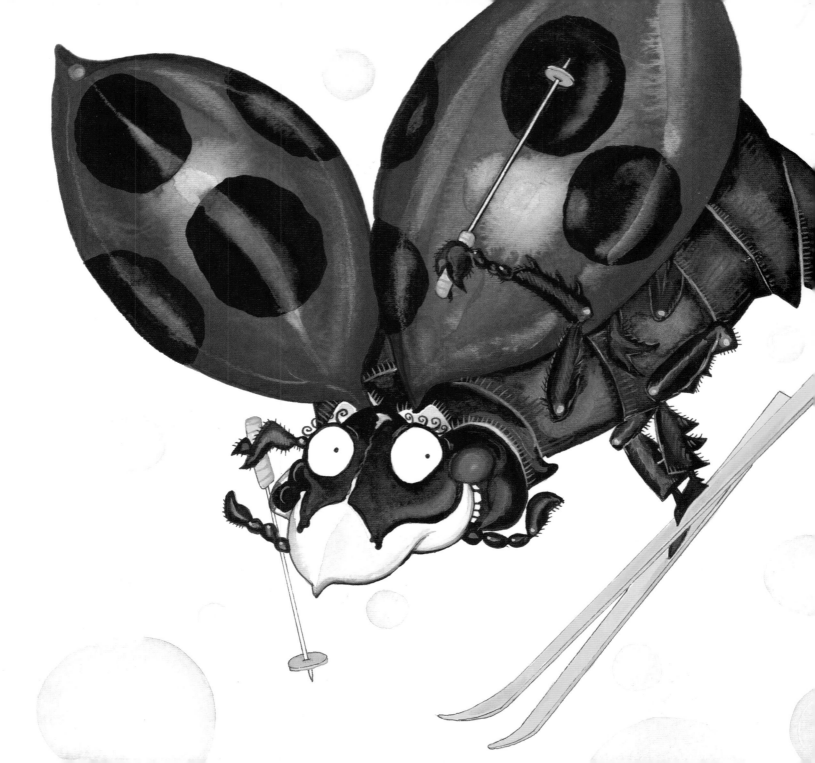

A beetle was singing

songs in the shower.

He must have been there

for over an hour.

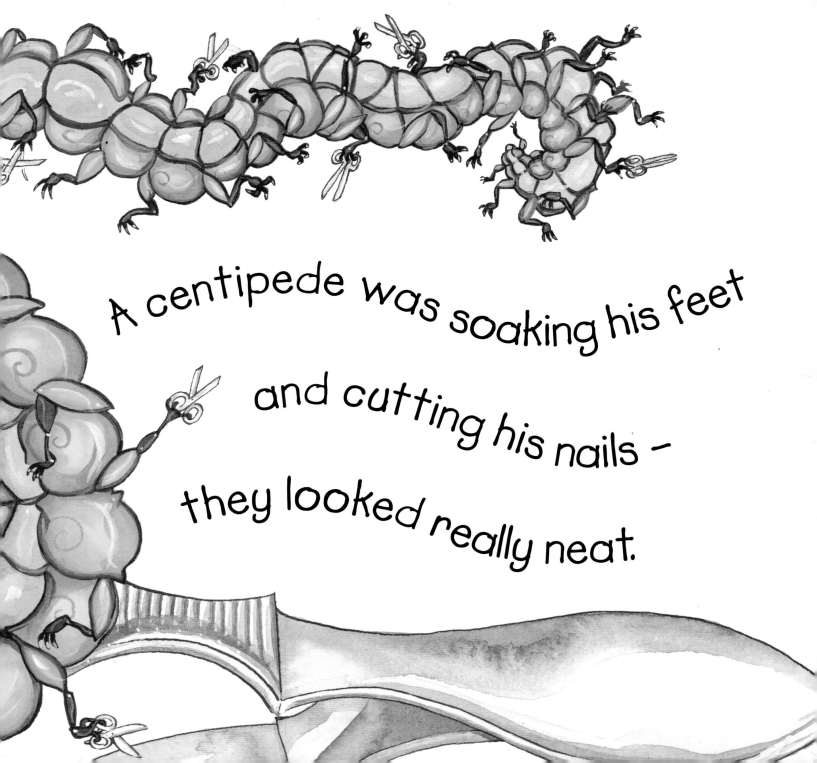

A centipede was soaking his feet
and cutting his nails –
they looked really neat.

A spider bungee jumped from the sink

where ants had discovered
a skating rink.

And by the mirror a butterfly was dabbing make-up around each eye.

And I was waiting to use the loo, so I shouted out,

Hey,

all of you...

... when you've all finished

sploshing and splashing,

slipping and sliding,
crashing and dashing,
shaving and waving and
misbehaving...

PLEASE?